VISUAL ANALYTICS

DR. REVA MISHRA

Copyright © Dr. Reva Mishra
All Rights Reserved.

This book is dedicated for the MBA and BBA students it will be mile stone for the Data Science students

Contents

Foreword   *vii*

Preface   *ix*

1. Getting Started With Data Visualization   1

2. Data Administration   5

3. The Visual Analytics Explorer   17

4. Designing Reports   33

5. Sas Visual Analytics Viewer   36

6. Data Visualzation Through Tablue   41

Foreword

It were well could one of the Men I have painted take up the pen and contribute a character sketch of the "man who has painted me" By the God grace i got an opportunity to write a book on the topic Visual Analytics for the MBa Aspirants those who want to make their career in the field of Data Science.

I Wish Good Luck.....

Sincere Regards

Dr Reva Mishra

Preface

The moto of the book is to promote data visulisation upto the end user to make better decision making. Whereas this book deals with six chapter which clearly shows the need and the demand for the growth and the development of the data mining and warehousing..

Author.....,

CHAPTER ONE

GETTING STARTED WITH DATA VISUALIZATION

What is Visual Analytics?

Visual analytics is the use of sophisticated tools and processes to analyze datasets using visual representations of the data. Visualizing the data in graphs, charts, and maps helps users identify patterns and thereby develop actionable insights. These insights help organizations make better, data-driven decisions.

Visual Analytics Benefits

Sometimes confused with data visualization, visual analytics isn't simply a matter of representing data graphically. Modern, interactive visual analytics makes it easy to combine data from multiple sources and deeply analyze the data directly within the visualization itself. Plus, AI and machine learning algorithms can offer recommendations to help guide your exploration.Ultimately, visual analytics helps you turn massive data sets into business insights which can have a major positive impact on your organization.

1.Share findings and track progress: Interactive reports and dashboards help users track, organize and share key performance indicators across an organization.

2.Make faster decisions: Users can understand data insights much more quickly by seeing and working with data sets when they are in a visual format.

3.Explore data more easily: Self-service analytics tools which allow users to interact with data in a visual context allows them to discover hidden relationships and patterns in the data without relying on help from IT.

4.Promote data literacy: Making data easier to work with and understand democratizes data analytics, getting more people across and organization involved.

Visual Analytics Examples

Explore these examples based on KPIs relevant to specific roles.

Marketing

In this example, visual analytics helps a marketer boost ROI by letting them see and understand each phase of the customer life cycle. This is made possible by connecting data from the CRM, advertising tools, and web analytics platform.

Supply Chain

Big data visual analytics can help supply chain managers immediately find connections between complex, disparate data sources by surfacing KPIs and allowing interactive exploration.

Sales

Sales managers benefit from the clean, organized presentation of sales data to increase revenue, improve forecasting, and identify key trends.

Human Resources

Visualizations can provide HR executives the ability to review and analyze KPIs in a single dashboard. This example shows data on employees by role and by location, plus key data such as gender ratio and training progress.

Finance

In this example, a loan manager at a consumer bank can explore how different regions, product and loan officers perform over time and drive the biggest impact on revenue and margins.

IT Visual Analytics

IT managers can leverage data analytics and visualization to better anticipate upcoming technology needs and identify underused systems and applications.

v. Visual Analytics Best Practices

To help you be successful with visual analytics, we've compiled the following key best practices to be aware of.

1.Define goals

Before you begin, be sure to define specific goals for your visual data analysis work. What specific questions are you trying to answer?

2.Integrate and manage the data

Your source data needs to be transformed into clean, business-ready information. You'll need to combine and replicate data from a variety of sources and then bring it into standardized formats stored in a repository such as a data lake or data warehouse.

3.Simplify visualizations

Choose the right visual technique to present your story in the simplest way possible. Learn more about visualizing data.

4.Get Inspired

See the ten most compelling and interesting data visualization examples from recent years.

<u>**Visual Analytics Software Capabilities**</u>

With so many vendors offering visualization features as part of their software, it can be difficult to select the right tool to meet your needs. The best data analytics tools include the following capabilities:

1.Integrate and manage big data

The best tools can combine and manage data from multiple sources to give users the full picture.

2.Allow free exploration

Your tool should allow you to freely explore data in whatever direction your intuition leads. Static charts and linear drill-downs make it harder to answer your questions.

3.Suggest visuals with AI

Augmented analytics recommends visualizations which help even novice users build their own analytics views and discover hidden insights.

4.Embed everywhere

Your software should let users explore visual data analysis from within whatever websites, portals, apps and business processes they use to make decisions.

A Glimpse of some FAQ's

<u>**What's the difference between data visualization and visual analytics?**</u>

The term data visualization typically refers to the graphical depiction of data, or representing data in bubble charts, heat maps, and other visuals to help people better understand the patterns, relationships, trends, and other meaningful insights in datasets. Visual analytics refers to the use of an analytics program to perform advanced analysis of complex datasets and allow users to explore and interact with dynamic visualizations.

<u>**Why is visual analytics important?**</u>

It is important because it allows users without data science skills or experience to combine, manipulate, and explore large, dynamic, multi-dimensional, and multi-sourced datasets. In a world in which big data becomes the norm, visual analytics becomes an essential tool.

How do you use visual analytics for business intelligence?

Business users can leverage visual analytics to more easily explore and understand large volumes of diverse data and gather the insights they need to solve problems, identify key opportunities, optimize performance, and inform strategic and tactical decision-making. It can also be used to create interactive dashboards and support collaboration amongst teams working with the same datasets.

What are some methods used to visualize data?

Bar charts, line charts, pie charts, cartograms, donut charts, heat maps, histograms, radial maps, streamgraphs, scatter plots, timelines, treemaps, and word clouds are some of the many ways data can be presented visually.

What is the scope of visual analytics?

The emerging field of visual analytics focuses on handling these massive, heterogenous, and dynamic volumes of information by integrating human judgement by means of visual representations and interaction techniques in the analysis process.

What is the role of visualization in data science?

Data visualization helps to tell stories by curating data into a form easier to understand, highlighting the trends and outliers. A good visualization tells a story, removing the noise from data and highlighting the useful information.

Course environment & scenario

The Visual Analytics course helps Tableau users design visualizations that viewers can easily understand and use. This course uses Tableau to develop and discuss visualizations, but does not include instruction on how to use Tableau products—we expect that you already know how to navigate and use Tableau.

CHAPTER TWO

Data Administration

Data administration is the process by which data is monitored, maintained and managed by a data administrator and/or an organization. Data administration allows an organization to control its data assets, as well as their processing and interactions with different applications and business processes. Data administration ensures that the entire life cycle of data use and processing is on par with the enterprise's objective.

Data administration may also be called data resource management.

1. Dictionary
2. Data Management
3. Data Administration

Data Administration

What Does Data Administration Mean?

Data administration is the process by which data is monitored, maintained and managed by a data administrator and/or an organization. Data administration allows an organization to control its data assets, as well as their processing and interactions with different applications and business processes. Data administration ensures that the entire life cycle of data use and processing is on par with the enterprise's objective.

Data administration may also be called data resource management.

Techopedia Explains Data Administration

Data administration typically involves the logical management of data in which the flow of data is analyzed, data models are created and the relationships among them are defined. Data administration also defines the security and access control elements of data where executive level data might be limited to some people and processes.

Data management differs from database administration in that the former defines the processes used to manage and maintain data as an organizational asset, whereas the latter deals with the technicalities involved with managing and distributing data.

DATA BUILDING

Having a good database of potential buyers is important for any marketing team to pursue and increase the sales figures. The more the number of potential buyers in the database, the more real time options the business has to perform well. This information of potential buyers is picked up from the various data sources and analysing them on using different variables.

However, building up such a database involves lot of effort of time and energy. Many times, the effort involved would be much more than the actual benefit. Hence it is important to have the right process and protocols in place for data building which would help to ease up the whole process.

Data building is a process which involves – Gathering information collating the same, diversifying and segmenting the data etc. Each of these steps requires a specific protocol to be followed to ensure the right quality database is build up.

We provide exclusive data building services which helps to have a ready database for your marketing team to pursue further. We have a Master file of B2B marketing data where the database runs into millions of records. All these records are unique and relevant. We have the prior permission of all the record holders for the data to be used. The higher relevancy of the data helps to ensure that you have the maximum possibility of finding a relevant record about who is interested in your product.

PROCESS

We follow a unique process for Data building , which includes :

- Researching and identifying the right sectors and industries
- Identifying the business organizations that need your services
- Identifying profiles relevant to you
- Collating the information
- Update the database with all the required details
- Verification checks on various levels for authenticity and consistency

Data building forms the base upon which the database can be updated regularly with relevant information.

What is Data Management?

Data management is the practice of collecting, organizing, protecting, and storing an organization's data so it can be analyzed for business decisions. As organizations create and consume data at unprecedented rates, data management solutions become essential for making sense of the vast quantities of data. Today's leading data management software ensures that reliable, up-to-date data is always used to drive decisions. The software helps with everything from data preparation to cataloging, search, and governance, allowing people to quickly find the information they need for analysis.

Types of Data Management

Data management plays several roles in an organization's data environment, making essential functions easier and less time-intensive. These data management techniques include the following:

- Data preparation is used to clean and transform raw data into the right shape and format for analysis, including making corrections and combining data sets.
- Data pipelines enable the automated transfer of data from one system to another.
- ETLs (Extract, Transform, Load) are built to take the data from one system, transform it, and load it into the organization's data warehouse.
- Data catalogs help manage metadata to create a complete picture of the data, providing a summary of its changes, locations, and quality while also making the data easy to find.
- Data warehouses are places to consolidate various data sources, contend with the many data types businesses store, and provide a clear route for data analysis.

- Data governance defines standards, processes, and policies to maintain data security and integrity.
- Data architecture provides a formal approach for creating and managing data flow.
- Data security protects data from unauthorized access and corruption.
- Data modeling documents the flow of data through an application or organization.

Why data management is important

Data management is a crucial first step to employing effective data analysis at scale, which leads to important insights that add value to your customers and improve your bottom line. With effective data management, people across an organization can find and access trusted data for their queries. Some benefits of an effective data management solution include:

- **Visibility**

Data management can increase the visibility of your organization's data assets, making it easier for people to quickly and confidently find the right data for their analysis. Data visibility allows your company to be more organized and productive, allowing employees to find the data they need to better do their jobs.

- **Reliability**

Data management helps minimize potential errors by establishing processes and policies for usage and building trust in the data being used to make decisions across your organization. With reliable, up-to-date data, companies can respond more efficiently to market changes and customer needs.

- **Security**

Data management protects your organization and its employees from data losses, thefts, and breaches with authentication and encryption tools. Strong data security ensures that vital company information is backed up and retrievable should the primary source become unavailable. Additionally, security becomes more and more important if your data contains any personally identifiable information that needs to be carefully managed to comply with consumer protection laws.

- **Scalability**

Data management allows organizations to effectively scale data and usage occasions with repeatable processes to keep data and metadata up to date. When processes are easy to repeat, your organization can avoid the unnecessary costs of duplication, such as employees conducting the same research over and over again or re-running costly queries unnecessarily.

What is Data Exploration?

Data exploration is the initial step in data analysis, where users explore a large data set in an unstructured way to uncover initial patterns, characteristics, and points of interest. This process isn't meant to reveal every bit of information a dataset holds, but rather to help create a broad picture of important trends and major points to study in greater detail.

Data exploration can use a combination of manual methods and automated tools such as data visualizations, charts, and initial reports.

This process makes deeper analysis easier because it can help target future searches and begin the process of excluding irrelevant data points and search paths that may turn up no results. More importantly, it helps build a familiarity with the existing information that makes finding better answers much simpler.

Many times, data exploration uses visualization because it creates a more straightforward view of data sets than simply examining thousands of individual numbers or names.

In any data exploration, the manual and automated aspects also look at different sides of the same coin. Manual analysis helps users familiarize themselves with information and can point to broad trends.

Deep Data Exploration – Advanced Analytics and Insights Using Python and R:

These methods are also by definition unstructured so that users can examine a whole set without any preconceptions. Automated tools, on the other hand, are excellent at pruning out less applicable data points, reorganizing data into sets that are easier to analyze, and scrubbing data sets to make their findings relevant.

What Can I Use Data Exploration For?

In any situation where you have a massive set of information, data exploration can help cut it down to a manageable size and focus efforts to optimize your analysis.

Most data analytics software includes visualization tools and charting features that make exploration at the outset significantly easier, helping reduce data by rooting out information that isn't required, or which can distort results in the long run.

By taking the time to perform a real exploration of your data along with visualization tools, you can also start finding correlations, patterns, and determine if a certain path is worth researching, or if the information is less usable.

Data exploration can also assist by reducing work time and finding more useful and actionable insights from the start alongside presenting clear paths to perform better analysis.

Deep Data Exploration – Advanced Analytics and Insights Using Python and R:

Table of Contents

- Advanced Analytics and Insights Using Python and R
- The Rise of Machine Learning and Predictive Analytics
- Advanced Statistical Analysis
- Go Beyond Quantitative Data with NLP
- Creating Complex Visuals with Python and R
- Data Cleaning
- Powerful Data Transformations
- Deeper Analysis and Enhanced Insights with Python and R in Sisense for Cloud Data Teams

Advanced Analytics and Insights Using Python and R

Modern data teams are laser-focused on maximizing the effectiveness of data analysis and the value of the insights that they uncover. The challenge of achieving these goals is only intensifying when faced with the escalating volume of data and the increasing variety of its sources. Success involves data teams exploring data as deeply as possible, extracting and analyzing the best quality data, and employing technologies and techniques that enable them to take the fullest advantage of the data they collect. The key to this success is choosing a platform that supports the programming languages that can evolve and enable the team to prepare data and create value with new types of analysis.

Platforms that let analysts utilize advanced programming languages, such as Python and R, can do much more than counterparts that rely on SQL alone. They enable users to benefit from new, more sophisticated developments such as machine learning, natural language processing, and the latest advances in data cleaning. Most significantly, they allow users to analyze data more deeply than ever, identify answers to questions that would have been impossible to ask using just SQL, and find insights that weren't previously achievable.

That's why Sisense for Cloud Data Teams includes support for Python and R. Integrating these two languages into our product gives companies a much more efficient way to manage their current data processes and brand new abilities to analyze data at brand new depths. In this paper, we'll discuss some of these new abilities to help your team see the value of incorporating new languages into your data workflow.

- **The Rise of Machine Learning and Predictive Analytics**

Predictive analytics and the importance of clean data

Traditionally, you would use your BI and analytics platform to analyze existing trends, identify backward-looking behaviors and respond to them. But you don't have to stop there. Machine learning enables you to identify and predict outcomes that can influence your organization's strategy. This ability is extremely helpful, but it depends heavily on having complete, reliable, "clean" data. Advanced programming languages help you clean your data far better than outdated, static languages, so you can be more confident that you have a strong foundation for making forward-thinking decisions.

- **Machine learning in Sisense for Cloud Data Teams with Python and R**

In order to identify complex patterns in current datasets, you need sophisticated tools, and that's what Python and R offer. Machine learning really comes into its own when these languages are used to apply algorithms to huge volumes of existing or past data and then extrapolate those patterns onto new inputs to predict potential outcomes: in other words, find trends in existing data and anticipate how they will impact new data.

Integrating Python and R into the Sisense for Cloud Data Teams platform gives you expanded data cleaning and analysis abilities that will streamline the creation of new machine learning models. If you can rely on having large, clean datasets, you can be confident about the means with which you can predict new trends with that data. The result is added value in the form of more accurate machine learning models. Since the models train on existing data, the benefits of clean data also compound into smarter, faster predictions in the future.

- **Advanced Statistical Analysis**

Organizations are becoming increasingly data-driven to stay ahead of the competition, and they can now do it with the help of predictive analytics, aided by advanced programming languages.

It's a virtuous circle. Organizations need to go beyond making decisions based exclusively on previous results. They want to confidently predict outcomes and make decisions based on those predictions. SQL alone can't do this it's more of a descriptive language that's only good at explaining what's happening. R and Python allow teams to answer questions about why something is happening and what is going to happen next. Those languages can be used to identify patterns that correlate with potential outcomes far more efficiently, often in just a single line. The example below shows the difference between the way SQL determines a correlation between just two variables, and the same type of function written in R, which can analyze many relationships at once in a large matrix of data.

- **Creating Complex Visuals with Python and R**

With all this advanced data comes the challenge of presenting it clearly. You can only realize the potential of deep data analysis if the results are easily understandable by as many people as possible within your organization, particularly the decision-makers who may not have technical know-how. It stands to reason that complex data requires tools that can handle visualizing complex results and concepts.

Traditionally, using simple visuals, analysts have developed charts showing multiple results by creating each layer and then stacking them together into a single visual. It's a slow and limited process that's extremely hard to scale efficiently. Python and R expedite this process because they have comprehensive charting libraries that enable you to visualize many results at once and show the interrelations between them. This makes it far easier to do deep analysis and meets a practical customer need.

Some visuals are designed to tell multiple stories, especially the more complex ones. Consider the chart below, which displays the mileage performance of vehicles with different engine types. A first look would illustrate that vehicles with fewer cylinders in the engine would appear to get better overall mileage while driving in the city. But there's more to this chart: the 8-cylinder engine has a unique shape that needs explanation, the 4-cylinder engine has a long tail while the other two have definite limits and there's a peculiar bimodal distribution in all three.

This chart can be examined for more findings, but it's clear that the complete story this data is telling goes deeper than anything that could be derived from simple tables or bar charts.

As growing volumes and types of data have become more rapidly available, customers increasingly want more options to build new charts. With Python and R, you get the capability to develop your own visualizations and dashboards, and customize them however you want, in ways that aren't limited by a fixed set of options or the need for technical experts to build one-off charts. The Sisense for Cloud Data Teams platform includes over 25 charting libraries to help you customize your visualizations, and the number of options will grow as both languages develop further. This enhances your ability to demonstrate results creatively, clearly, and comprehensibly. Consequently, it makes the results of the data more accessible, so understanding these results is simpler, and the path to achieving more insights gets smoother. Quite literally, we're giving power to you, the builders. Furthermore, the ability you gain with Python and R to visualize complex data means you now have the capability to tell richer stories than you can with standard, basic data.

- **Data Cleaning**

In order to get great insights from your data, you need to be sure that what you're analyzing is accurate and relevant: in short, "clean". There's no point wasting precious time, effort, and resources on "dirty" data such as unnecessary duplication, inaccuracies, or out-of-date information. It'll only hinder your business and it's expensive. It's estimated that this can cost companies as much as 12% of overall revenue, amounting to $3.1 trillion wasted each year in the US alone.

To compound the problem, it has been acknowledged that data scientists spend around 80% of their time preparing and managing data for analysis. Most of this time involves cleaning and organizing data, leaving just a small proportion for analysis and adding value. Besides being arduous and wasteful, it makes data teams disgruntled because 76% of them consider data preparation to be the least enjoyable part of their work.

It's hugely welcome that advanced coding languages like Python and R can help expedite the data cleaning process since they include packages that enable data teams to perform bulk cleanup. With Sisense for Cloud Data Teams, the data is taken from SQL and passed into one of these languages for editing and bulk cleanup in just a fraction of the time it would normally take.

For example, Python's re library makes string operations much faster and simpler than using SQL for the same action, dramatically reducing the amount of time and effort that goes into cleaning. Consider a dataset with a lot of missing data. Built-in Pandas functions such as fillna and dropna allow data scientists to treat all empty cells in a range the same way. Those cells can be filled with the mean, median, or specific values (fillna) or removed entirely (dropna). Other large-scale cleanup activities like removing duplicates can also be handled with individual lines of code rather than the time-intensive processes that must be used to complete the same task in SQL.

As a result, the data cleaning process becomes much more efficient, so analysts can spend less time and fewer resources on it, and more time doing what they're good at: namely research and analysis that result in strong insights that add real value to your organization

Powerful Data Transformations

Once data has been cleaned and analyzed, you can analyze and generate insights. In order to maximize the impact of these insights, it's important that they're understood by as many people as possible within your organization. This involves the critical process of turning data tables into visualizations, and once again, using Python and R makes the process easier, faster, and more effective than just using SQL.

- **How Python and R make this easier**

In SQL, queries can be run to produce tables, but if you want to create charts, you'll need to pass these queries into a BI platform like Sisense for Cloud Data Teams. This means data is being prepared in one environment and then visualized in another. Moving the data in this way, you may risk losing some of the formatting in translation. On the other hand, Python and R are set up for data visualization. For instance, Python enables you to pivot (spread) or melt (gather) data, and R has spread and gather functions in a library like Tidyr that makes it easy to map data, manipulate and restructure data tables within a single environment. In the two images below, pivoting changes the data from the image on the left to look like the image on the right. Melting does the opposite.

Also, Python speeds up the analysis and plotting of data by converting object datatypes into category types that don't need anywhere near as much memory to manipulate the data and visualize it.

Restructuring Data in Sisense for Cloud Data Teams

Sisense for Cloud Data Teams makes it easy to reformat data tables in advanced languages. Just run a SQL query to process the dataset, then pass the table into R or Python and use the reshape2/ tidyR or pandas libraries to execute the transformation with a simple command. Using just SQL, manipulations like this would take multiple lines of complex transposing code. In some cases, queries that would take 50-100 lines to perform and run in SQL can be managed in R or Python with just a single line.

Once the data has been transformed, R and Python offer more advanced charting libraries that can create complex, customized visuals for data teams. Visuals that have been created to fit the specifications and preferences of key stakeholders; data teams can pass them directly into Sisense for Cloud Data Teams to be included in shared dashboards.

- **Deeper Analysis and Enhanced Insights with Python and R in Sisense for Cloud Data Teams**

We have seen how integrating Python and R into your BI and analytics platform takes your ability to analyze and visualize data to the next level.

The Sisense for Cloud Data Teams platform's support for these advanced coding languages opens the door to far more comprehensive and impactful insights and enables you to answer previously unanswerable questions. Even better, it can all be done simply and speedily. It's a true revolution in analytics.

CHAPTER THREE

THE VISUAL ANALYTICS EXPLORER

According to the SAS website, "It is an easy-to-use, web-based product that leverages SAS high-performance analytic technologies.

It empowers organizations to explore huge volumes of data very quickly to identify patterns, trends, and opportunities for further analysis."

In other words, it's USP is its ability to combine SAS' analytic technology with a seamless user interface and beautiful visual analytics. It is used by accounting and CPA firms, advertising agencies, banking institutions, manufacturing companies, government entities, and technology companies. It can be adapted to the industry it is being used in.

What are the Benefits of SAS Visual Analytics?

In traditional reporting, what you're reporting on and what needs to be conveyed is always known upfront. Therefore, it is more of a binary and linear process. With it, however, all that changes.

You can actually explore data and its relationships without any predefined goals and discover new insights using the powerful SAS analytics engine. SAS visual analytics tutorials and SAS visual analytics certifications help understand these benefits in more detail. Here are some of the major benefits:

1. You can share insights from it on both desktops as well as mobile.
2. Users can apply the power of SAS analytics to massive amounts of data.
3. Users can explore data visually at very high speeds.
4. Users can create powerful statistics models by using SAS visual statistics.
5. It allows you to create visual reports and dashboards based on ordinary tables and graphs.
6. The tool allows users to create customized graphs quickly.

7. It has the ability to connect with all third parties and merge their data in one system. It then analyzes the structured information in a consistent and reliable manner.
8. The software is widely used across the IT industry since it has a diverse set of analytics tools.
9. It is a very intuitive software, especially when compared to similar tools in the market.

Viewing Reports on Mobile Devices

Because the report viewer is not supported on mobile devices, mobile users are redirected to the SAS Visual Analytics App when opening a report. The SAS Visual Analytics Apps (formerly called SAS Mobile BI) are free mobile apps

About SAS Visual Analytics App

SAS Visual Analytics App enables you to view and interact with SAS Visual Analytics reports on your mobile device. You can also share observations with others while on the go. The SAS Visual Analytics App (previously called SAS Mobile BI) supports all charts and graphs that are available in SAS Visual Analytics.

A single application for reporting, data exploration and analytics

See the big picture – and underlying connections.

Quickly spot important relationships in your data using suggestions and clearly identified related measures. Use machine learning and natural language explanations to find, visualize and narrate stories and insights that are easy to understand and explain. Find out why something happened, examine all options and uncover opportunities hidden deep in your data. Automatically highlight key relationships, outliers, clusters and more to reveal vital insights that inspire action.

SAS Visual Analytics on SAS Viya
showing visual data exploration on
desktop monitor

Turn seeing into understanding with dynamic visuals.

Create stunning interactive reports and dashboards. Quickly summarize
key performance metrics and share them via the web and mobile devices.
Executives and front-line staff can quickly interact with and collaborate
on insights, slice and dice them to find their own answers, and better
understand business performance.

SAS Visual Analytics on SAS Viya
showing interactive reports on
desktop monitor

Get answers backed by data, results driven by insight.

Easy-to-use predictive analytics enables even business analysts to assess
possible outcomes and make smarter, data-driven decisions – no
programming required. Smart algorithms reduce the need for manual
experimentation. And you can work collaboratively with experts to focus
on what's most relevant.

SAS Visual Analytics on SAS Viya
showing self service analytics on desktop
monitor

Add the 'where' to the 'what.'

Add geographical context to your analyses and visualizations by combining traditional data with location data. Location analysis brings the "where" dimension to the forefront so you can analyze data in new ways to get the full picture before making decisions while identifying location-specific opportunities.

SAS Visual Analytics on SAS Viya
showing location analytics

Streamline the discovery process.

Self-service data preparation gives business users the ability to import their own data, join tables, apply data quality functions, create calculated columns and more – all with drag-and-drop ease. By empowering users to access, combine, clean and prepare their own data in an agile – and trusted – way, SAS Visual Analytics facilitates faster, broader adoption of analytics for your entire organization.

SAS Visual Analytics on SAS Viya showing self service data preparation shown on desktop monitor

What is SAS Visual Analytics?

According to the SAS website, "It is an easy-to-use, web-based product that leverages SAS high-performance analytic technologies.

It empowers organizations to explore huge volumes of data very quickly to identify patterns, trends, and opportunities for further analysis."

In other words, it's USP is its ability to combine SAS' analytic technology with a seamless user interface and beautiful visual analytics. It is used by accounting and CPA firms, advertising agencies, banking institutions, manufacturing companies, government entities, and technology companies. It can be adapted to the industry it is being used in.

According

Sas visual analytics. Source blogs. Sas. Com

How does SAS Visual Analytics Work?

It starts with the process of exploring and viewing the data in different ways. Users then use the tool to derive insights from their data and create models and reports based on these insights. These reports are also visually rich and easy to interpret.

Here are the steps involved:

1. **Explore the data.** You can use visualization to understand and explore the raw data.

2. **Build analytics models.** You can build predictive models using the raw data and generate model outputs.
3. **Create reports.** You can design your reports and dashboard to be as visually appealing as you want. You can also schedule and distribute your reports directly through the tool. The reports can be viewed both on the web and on mobile devices.

Working

Here's an infographic that describes the various elements involved and exactly how it works.

According to the SAS website, "It is an easy-to-use, web-based product that leverages SAS high-performance analytic technologies.

It empowers organizations to explore huge volumes of data very quickly to identify patterns, trends, and opportunities for further analysis."

In other words, it's USP is its ability to combine SAS' analytic technology with a seamless user interface and beautiful <u>visual analytics</u>. It is used by accounting and CPA firms, advertising agencies, banking institutions, manufacturing companies, government entities, and technology companies. It can be adapted to the industry it is being used in.

What are the Benefits of SAS Visual Analytics?

In traditional reporting, what you're reporting on and what needs to be conveyed is always known upfront. Therefore, it is more of a binary and linear process. With it, however, all that changes.

You can actually explore data and its relationships without any predefined goals and discover new insights using the powerful SAS analytics engine. SAS visual analytics tutorials and SAS visual analytics certifications help understand these benefits in more detail. Here are some of the major benefits:

1. You can share insights from it on both desktops as well as mobile.
2. Users can apply the power of SAS analytics to massive amounts of data.
3. Users can explore data visually at very high speeds.
4. Users can create powerful statistics models by using SAS visual statistics.
5. It allows you to create visual reports and dashboards based on ordinary tables and graphs.
6. The tool allows users to create customized graphs quickly.
7. It has the ability to connect with all third parties and merge their data in one system. It then analyzes the structured information in a consistent and reliable manner.
8. The software is widely used across the IT industry since it has a diverse set of analytics tools.
9. It is a very intuitive software, especially when compared to similar tools in the market.

Viewing Reports on Mobile Devices

Because the report viewer is not supported on mobile devices, mobile users are redirected to the SAS Visual Analytics App when opening a report. The SAS Visual Analytics Apps (formerly called SAS Mobile BI) are free mobile apps

About SAS Visual Analytics App

SAS Visual Analytics App enables you to view and interact with SAS Visual Analytics reports on your mobile device. You can also share observations with others while on the go. The SAS Visual Analytics App (previously called SAS Mobile BI) supports all charts and graphs that are available in SAS Visual Analytics.

A single application for reporting, data exploration and analytics

See the big picture – and underlying connections.

Quickly spot important relationships in your data using suggestions and clearly identified related measures. Use machine learning and natural language explanations to find, visualize and narrate stories and insights that are easy to understand and explain. Find out why something happened, examine all options and uncover opportunities hidden deep in your data. Automatically highlight key relationships, outliers, clusters and more to reveal vital insights that inspire action.

Turn seeing into understanding with dynamic visuals.

Create stunning interactive reports and dashboards. Quickly summarize key performance metrics and share them via the web and mobile devices. Executives and front-line staff can quickly interact with and collaborate on insights, slice and dice them to find their own answers, and better understand business performance.

Get answers backed by data, results driven by insight.

Easy-to-use predictive analytics enables even business analysts to assess possible outcomes and make smarter, data-driven decisions – no programming required. Smart algorithms reduce the need for manual experimentation. And you can work collaboratively with experts to focus on what's most relevant.

Add the 'where' to the 'what.'

Add geographical context to your analyses and visualizations by combining traditional data with location data. Location analysis brings the "where" dimension to the forefront so you can analyze data in new ways to get the full picture before making decisions while identifying location-specific opportunities.

Streamline the discovery process.

Self-service data preparation gives business users the ability to import their own data, join tables, apply data quality functions, create calculated columns and more – all with drag-and-drop ease. By empowering

users to access, combine, clean and prepare their own data in an agile – and trusted – way, SAS Visual Analytics facilitates faster, broader adoption of analytics for your entire organization.

SAS Visual Analytics on SAS Viya showing self service data preparation shown on desktop monitor

What is SAS Visual Analytics?

According to the SAS website, "It is an easy-to-use, web-based product that leverages SAS high-performance analytic technologies.

It empowers organizations to explore huge volumes of data very quickly to identify patterns, trends, and opportunities for further analysis."

In other words, it's USP is its ability to combine SAS' analytic technology with a seamless user interface and beautiful visual analytics. It is used by accounting and CPA firms, advertising agencies, banking institutions, manufacturing companies, government entities, and technology companies.

It can be adapted to the industry it is being used in.

According

How does SAS Visual Analytics Work?

It starts with the process of exploring and viewing the data in different ways. Users then use the tool to derive insights from their data and create models and reports based on these insights. These reports are also visually rich and easy to interpret.

Here are the steps involved:

1. **Explore the data.** You can use visualization to understand and explore the raw data.
2. **Build analytics models.** You can build predictive models using the raw data and generate model outputs.
3. **Create reports.** You can design your reports and dashboard to be as visually appealing as you want. You can also schedule and distribute your reports directly through the tool. The reports can be viewed both on the web and on mobile devices.Working

Here's an infographic that describes the various elements involved and exactly how it works.

According to the SAS website, "It is an easy-to-use, web-based product that leverages SAS high-performance analytic technologies.

It empowers organizations to explore huge volumes of data very quickly to identify patterns, trends, and opportunities for further analysis."

In other words, it's USP is its ability to combine SAS' analytic technology with a seamless user interface and beautiful visual analytics. It is used by accounting and CPA firms, advertising agencies, banking institutions, manufacturing companies, government entities, and technology companies. It can be adapted to the industry it is being used in.

What are the Benefits of SAS Visual Analytics?

In traditional reporting, what you're reporting on and what needs to be conveyed is always known upfront. Therefore, it is more of a binary and linear process. With it, however, all that changes.

You can actually explore data and its relationships without any predefined goals and discover new insights using the powerful SAS analytics engine. SAS visual analytics tutorials and SAS visual analytics certifications help understand these benefits in more detail. Here are some of the major benefits:

1. You can share insights from it on both desktops as well as mobile.
2. Users can apply the power of SAS analytics to massive amounts of data.
3. Users can explore data visually at very high speeds.
4. Users can create powerful statistics models by using SAS visual statistics.
5. It allows you to create visual reports and dashboards based on ordinary tables and graphs.
6. The tool allows users to create customized graphs quickly.
7. It has the ability to connect with all third parties and merge their data in one system. It then analyzes the structured information in a consistent and reliable manner.
8. The software is widely used across the IT industry since it has a diverse set of analytics tools.
9. It is a very intuitive software, especially when compared to similar tools in the market.

Viewing Reports on Mobile Devices

Because the report viewer is not supported on mobile devices, mobile users are redirected to the SAS Visual Analytics App when opening a report. The SAS Visual Analytics Apps (formerly called SAS Mobile BI) are free mobile apps

About SAS Visual Analytics App

SAS Visual Analytics App enables you to view and interact with SAS Visual Analytics reports on your mobile device. You can also share observations with others while on the go. The SAS Visual Analytics App (previously called SAS Mobile BI) supports all charts and graphs that are available in SAS Visual Analytics.

A single application for reporting, data exploration and analytics

See the big picture – and underlying connections.

Quickly spot important relationships in your data using suggestions and clearly identified related measures. Use machine learning and natural language explanations to find, visualize and narrate stories and insights that are easy to understand and explain. Find out why something happened, examine all options and uncover opportunities hidden deep in your data. Automatically highlight key relationships, outliers, clusters and more to reveal vital insights that inspire action.

SAS Visual Analytics on SAS Viya showing visual data exploration on desktop monitor

Turn seeing into understanding with dynamic visuals.

Create stunning interactive reports and dashboards. Quickly summarize key performance metrics and share them via the web and mobile devices. Executives and front-line staff can quickly interact with and collaborate on insights, slice and dice them to find their own answers, and better understand business performance.

Get answers backed by data, results driven by insight.

Easy-to-use predictive analytics enables even business analysts to assess possible outcomes and make smarter, data-driven decisions – no programming required. Smart algorithms reduce the need for manual experimentation. And you can work collaboratively with experts to focus on what's most relevant.

Add the 'where' to the 'what.'

Add geographical context to your analyses and visualizations by combining traditional data with location data. Location analysis brings the "where" dimension to the forefront so you can analyze data in new ways to get the full picture before making decisions while identifying location-specific opportunities.

Streamline the discovery process.

Self-service data preparation gives business users the ability to import their own data, join tables, apply data quality functions, create calculated columns and more – all with drag-and-drop ease. By empowering

users to access, combine, clean and prepare their own data in an agile – and trusted – way, SAS Visual Analytics facilitates faster, broader adoption of analytics for your entire organization.

SAS Visual Analytics on SAS Viya showing self service data preparation shown on desktop monitor

What is SAS Visual Analytics?

According to the SAS website, "It is an easy-to-use, web-based product that leverages SAS high-performance analytic technologies.

It empowers organizations to explore huge volumes of data very quickly to identify patterns, trends, and opportunities for further analysis."

In other words, it's USP is its ability to combine SAS' analytic technology with a seamless user interface and beautiful visual analytics. It is used by accounting and CPA firms, advertising agencies, banking institutions, manufacturing companies, government entities, and technology companies. It can be adapted to the industry it is being used in.

According

How does SAS Visual Analytics Work?

It starts with the process of exploring and viewing the data in different ways. Users then use the tool to derive insights from their data and create models and reports based on these insights. These reports are also visually rich and easy to interpret.

Here are the steps involved:

1. **Explore the data.** You can use visualization to understand and explore the raw data.
2. **Build analytics models.** You can build predictive models using the raw data and generate model outputs.
3. **Create reports.** You can design your reports and dashboard to be as visually appealing as you want. You can also schedule and distribute your reports directly through the tool. The reports can be viewed both on the web and on mobile devices.Working Here's an infographic that describes the various elements involved and exactly how it works.

CHAPTER FOUR

DESIGNING REPORTS

The Basics of Report Designing

Before designing the reports, the most important is to understand users' demands, which is the basis of designing the reports. You can use '5W1H' to refine the requirements.

Why- Why designing this report?

What- What information this report need to cover?

Who- Who are the end-users?

When- When reading these reports? (The frequency and the regular time)

Where- Where to publish and put this report?

How- How to design this report?

Report Design Guidelines

Clarify the report topic and KPIs

The core of the reports can be KPIs or some critical points in the project. These can be called the report topic.

One of the report tasks is to "paint a picture" of a business topic with multiple associated metrics with a hierarchy. Take this as the first step when you start report designing.

e.g., If the topic is 'income,' the reports will involve the source of revenue, what factors affect income, income trends, whether KPI of the cycle can be achieved.

e.g., If you focus on user growth, you can sort through the user categories, the key metrics of each AARRR phases, the results of products or operational activities related to user growth, ROIs, and so on.

e.g., If you focus on the channel entry, you will pay attention to the metrics associated with channel quality such as traffic, conversion rates, user value.

Different business scenarios have different business topics. The key indicators and report structures will also be different. But the train of thought is similar:

What are the key metrics of KPIs to focus on in this scenario?

What factors influence these core indicators?

What links are involved in this scenario?

How end-users read or use data?

After sorting out these four questions, it will be clear the indicators under the report subject and the structure of reports.

Determine the source of the data

Which database are the data from? ERP database? CRM database? Enterprise data warehouse?

What type of database? Oracle? MySql? SQL Server? BW? Hana? Greenplum?

What database tables are the data from? What kind of join relationships are these tables?

Here, I would recommend you use report software to support multiple databases. For example, FineReport supports all popular databases and allows you to integrate data from different sources. Therefore, wherever your data is in, you can conveniently combine these data to have a comprehensive view.

Analyze the data on the report to correspond to the fields of the underlying database table

In this step, you should pay attention to:

The data on the report comes from which field of which table?

Whether the data is directly from the corresponding fields of the database table? Or whether it needs to be processed, such as string interception or date format conversion.

Determine the filtering criteria

There is a large amount of business data in the database; if no filtering standards are added, all the business data will be extracted by default. If the data volume is large, the front-end tools will crash, and the database may also be down. Therefore, data filtering criteria need to be added to control the data range during report preparation.

Most reports have time filtering conditions, such as annual reports that need to be filtered by year, a quarterly report by quarter, monthly reports by month.

Choose the elements to display the data.

How is the data presented in the report? Tables or charts?

If it is tabular, using the row to list, column to list, or cross to list?

If it is a chart report, using the pie chart, bar chart, line chart or some other charts?

CHAPTER FIVE

SAS Visual Analytics Viewer

SAS Visual Analytics Viewer (the report viewer) enables users who are not report designers to view a report using a web browser

According to the SAS website, "It is an easy-to-use, web-based product that leverages SAS high-performance analytic technologies.

It empowers organizations to explore huge volumes of data very quickly to identify patterns, trends, and opportunities for further analysis."

In other words, it's USP is its ability to combine SAS' analytic technology with a seamless user interface and beautiful visual analytics. It is used by accounting and CPA firms, advertising agencies, banking institutions, manufacturing companies, government entities, and technology companies. It can be adapted to the industry it is being used in.

What are the Benefits of SAS Visual Analytics?

In traditional reporting, what you're reporting on and what needs to be conveyed is always known upfront. Therefore, it is more of a binary and linear process. With it, however, all that changes.

You can actually explore data and its relationships without any predefined goals and discover new insights using the powerful SAS analytics engine. SAS visual analytics tutorials and SAS visual analytics certifications help understand these benefits in more detail. Here are some of the major benefits:

1. You can share insights from it on both desktops as well as mobile.
2. Users can apply the power of SAS analytics to massive amounts of data.
3. Users can explore data visually at very high speeds.
4. Users can create powerful statistics models by using SAS visual statistics.
5. It allows you to create visual reports and dashboards based on ordinary tables and graphs.
6. The tool allows users to create customized graphs quickly.

7. It has the ability to connect with all third parties and merge their data in one system. It then analyzes the structured information in a consistent and reliable manner.
8. The software is widely used across the IT industry since it has a diverse set of analytics tools.
9. It is a very intuitive software, especially when compared to similar tools in the market.

Viewing Reports on Mobile Devices

Because the report viewer is not supported on mobile devices, mobile users are redirected to the SAS Visual Analytics App when opening a report. The SAS Visual Analytics Apps (formerly called SAS Mobile BI) are free mobile apps

About SAS Visual Analytics App

SAS Visual Analytics App enables you to view and interact with SAS Visual Analytics reports on your mobile device. You can also share observations with others while on the go. The SAS Visual Analytics App (previously called SAS Mobile BI) supports all charts and graphs that are available in SAS Visual Analytics.

A single application for reporting, data exploration and analytics

See the big picture – and underlying connections.

Quickly spot important relationships in your data using suggestions and clearly identified related measures. Use machine learning and natural language explanations to find, visualize and narrate stories and insights that are easy to understand and explain. Find out why something happened, examine all options and uncover opportunities hidden deep in your data. Automatically highlight key relationships, outliers, clusters and more to reveal vital insights that inspire action.

Turn seeing into understanding with dynamic visuals.

Create stunning interactive reports and dashboards. Quickly summarize key performance metrics and share them via the web and mobile devices. Executives and front-line staff can quickly interact with and collaborate on insights, slice and dice them to find their own answers, and better understand business performance.

Get answers backed by data, results driven by insight.

Easy-to-use predictive analytics enables even business analysts to assess possible outcomes and make smarter, data-driven decisions – no programming required. Smart algorithms reduce the need for manual experimentation. And you can work collaboratively with experts to focus on what's most relevant.

Add the 'where' to the 'what.'

Add geographical context to your analyses and visualizations by combining traditional data with location data. Location analysis brings the "where" dimension to the forefront so you can analyze data in new ways to get the full picture before making decisions while identifying location-specific opportunities.

Streamline the discovery process.

Self-service data preparation gives business users the ability to import their own data, join tables, apply data quality functions, create calculated columns and more – all with drag-and-drop ease. By empowering

users to access, combine, clean and prepare their own data in an agile – and trusted – way, SAS Visual Analytics facilitates faster, broader adoption of analytics for your entire organization.

What is SAS Visual Analytics?

According to the SAS website, "It is an easy-to-use, web-based product that leverages SAS high-performance analytic technologies.

It empowers organizations to explore huge volumes of data very quickly to identify patterns, trends, and opportunities for further analysis."

In other words, it's USP is its ability to combine SAS' analytic technology with a seamless user interface and beautiful visual analytics. It is used by accounting and CPA firms, advertising agencies, banking institutions, manufacturing companies, government entities, and technology companies. It can be adapted to the industry it is being used in.

According

How does SAS Visual Analytics Work?

It starts with the process of exploring and viewing the data in different ways. Users then use the tool to derive insights from their data and create models and reports based on these insights. These reports are also visually rich and easy to interpret.

Here are the steps involved:

1. **Explore the data.** You can use visualization to understand and explore the raw data.
2. **Build analytics models.** You can build predictive models using the raw data and generate model outputs.
3. **Create reports.** You can design your reports and dashboard to be as visually appealing as you want. You can also schedule and distribute your reports directly through the tool. The reports can be viewed both on the web and on mobile devices.Working Here's an infographic that describes the various elements involved and exactly how it works.Infographic

Market Demand

recent study by MONEY and payscale.com found that SAS Analytics skills are the most valuable skills to have in today's job market. The study analyzed 54 million employee profiles across 350 industries to come up with a list of 21 valuable skills and SAS analytics topped the list.

Companies are understanding the power of analytics more and more. They have realized that they can now apply big data analytics specialization to almost any area of their business, from marketing to supply chain to customer service, to improve outcomes and optimize their business. However, the power of analytics can only be realized effectively if they employ people who can understand and use analytics tools to their full potential.

As a result, there is a great demand for SAS analytics professionals in today's market. As far as it is concerned, its first version was released back in 2013 and it has only seen consistent growth in adoption since then.

More and more companies are moving to it due to its seamless interface and visual representation. As a result, getting a SAS visual analytics certification is a great way to find a well-paying and challenging job. There are some places that you can get your certification at that also provide placement support. It's also important, of course, to be prepared for basic

<u>SAS related interview questions</u> before you start interviewing for positions.

Final Thoughts

In conclusion, one can say that SAS visual analytics is fast becoming the go-to analytics tool for companies across the world. If you want to build a career in analytics, learning SAS is definitely the way to go. It combines the power of SAS' analytics engine with a seamless interface, user experience, and great data visualization. It will continue to be the tool of choice especially as more and more companies are realising the potential of powerful analytics.

CHAPTER SIX

DATA VISUALZATION THROUGH TABLUE

IIINTRODUCTION

What Is Data Visualization?

Data visualization is the graphical representation of information and data. By using <u>visual elements like charts, graphs, and maps</u>, data visualization tools provide an accessible way to see and understand trends, outliers, and patterns in data.

In the world of Big Data, data visualization tools and technologies are essential to analyze massive amounts of information and make data-driven decisions.

Big Data is here and we need to know what it says

As the <u>"age of Big Data" kicks into high-gear</u>, visualization is an increasingly key tool to make sense of the trillions of rows of data generated every day. Data visualization helps to tell stories by curating data into a form easier to understand, highlighting the trends and outliers.

A good visualization tells a story, removing the noise from data and highlighting the useful information. However, it's not simply as easy as just dressing up a graph to make it look better or slapping on the "info" part of an infographic. Effective data visualization is a delicate balancing act between form and function. The plainest graph could be too boring to catch any notice or it make tell a powerful point; the most stunning visualization could utterly fail at conveying the right message or it could speak volumes. The data and the visuals need to work together, and there's an art to combining great analysis with great storytelling.

Common general types of data visualization:

• Charts

- Tables
- Graphs
- Maps
- Infographics
- Dashboards

More specific examples of methods to visualize data:

- Area Chart
- Bar Chart
- Box-and-whisker Plots
- Bubble Cloud
- Bullet Graph
- Cartogram
- Circle View
- Dot Distribution Map
- Gantt Chart
- Heat Map
- Highlight Table
- Histogram
- Matrix
- Network
- Polar Area
- Radial Tree
- Scatter Plot (2D or 3D)
- Streamgraph
- Text Tables
- Timeline
- Treemap
- Wedge Stack Graph
- Word Cloud
- And any mix-and-match combination in a dashboard!

Introduction to Tableau.

In this technologically digitally advanced world, businesses have to deal with a lot of unstructured, raw data. There are professionals who help organizations to extract valuable, meaningful insights from this massive amount of data. One such professional is a data analyst and their weapon is data visualization. Data visualization tools help in presenting any information in a manner that is visually appealing and is easy to understand the implications of the data and how to act on them clearly.

One of the most popular data Visualization tools is Tableau.

When we discuss data visualization tools tableau, it is widely used today by many organizations, nearly **63,251** of them. Tableau is easy to use because it has a **drag and drop interface**. While using tableau for data analysis, performing tasks like sorting, analyzing, and comparing, very fast and easily.

What is Tableau?

Tableau Software is one of the quickest developing Data Visualization apparatuses which is now being utilized in the BI business. It is the ideal approach to change or change the crude arrangement of data into an effectively reasonable configuration with zero specialized aptitudes and coding data.

Tableau Software is one of the quickest developing Data Visualization apparatuses which is now being utilized in the BI business. It is the ideal approach to change or change the crude arrangement of data into an effectively reasonable configuration with zero specialized aptitudes and coding data.

What is Tableau Used for?

Use of Tableau programming are recorded beneath:

- Tableau programming is utilized to interpret inquiries into Visualization.
- It is additionally utilized for overseeing metadata.
- Programming in Tableau imports data, all things considered and extended.
- For a non-specialized client, Tableau is a lifeline as it offers the office to make '**no-code**' data inquiries.

As far back as it was presented, this data representation device is utilized for the Business Intelligence industry. Associations like Amazon, Walmart, Accenture, Lenovo, etc generally use Tableau

How Does Tableau Work?

- The significant work of <u>Tableau programming</u> is to associate and concentrate the data put away in different spots. It can pull data from any stage. Tableau can separate data from any database, be it Excel, PDF, Oracle, or even Amazon Web Services.
- When Tableau is propelled, prepared data connectors are accessible which enables you to interface with any database.
- The data extricated can be associated live to the Tableau data motor, Tableau Desktop. This is the place a Data Analyst or a Data Engineer works with the data that was pulled up and creates representation. The made dashboards are imparted to clients as static records. The clients accepting dashboards see the records utilizing Tableau Reader.
- The data extricated from Tableau Desktop can be distributed to Tableau Server, which is a venture stage where joint effort, dispersion, administration, security model, and robotization highlights are upheld.

How Does Tableau Work?

- The significant work of <u>Tableau programming</u> is to associate and concentrate the data put away in different spots. It can pull data from any stage. Tableau can separate data from any database, be it Excel, PDF, Oracle, or even Amazon Web Services.
- When Tableau is propelled, prepared data connectors are accessible which enables you to interface with any database.
- The data extricated can be associated live to the Tableau data motor, Tableau Desktop. This is the place a <u>Data Analyst</u> or a Data Engineer works with the data that was pulled up and creates representation. The made dashboards are imparted to clients as static records. The clients accepting dashboards see the records utilizing Tableau Reader.
- The data extricated from Tableau Desktop can be distributed to Tableau Server, which is a venture stage where joint effort, dispersion, administration, security model, and robotization highlights are upheld. Utilizing Tableau Server, end clients can get to the records from all areas, be it a work area or a cell phone.

Why Opt for Data Visualization Tools Tableau?

For what reason do organizations in general advance over the limits of conventional composed, sound and video data sources and go for data envisioning devices? Doubtlessly the cutting edge human is undeniably further developed as to be influenced by a bright attractive picture. But then, mental research shows that 90% of all the data that individuals see originates from their feeling of sight. Furthermore, the less complex how the data is put, the higher the odds that it is prepared.

Changing systematic data into optical structure encourages its absorption and comprehension and permits it to reveal important data. This may work in support of organizations if they influence such a characteristic effectively, as it permits upgrading business forms and improving representatives' presentations.:

Advantages of using tableau for Data Visualization

* ***Ease of Use***

The instrument's natural way of making illustrations and an easy to use interface permits non-dev clients to use the essential application's usefulness without limit. Clients organize crude Data into infectious graphs in an intuitive manner, which encourages Data breaking down and wipes out the requirement for the assistance of an IT office for design building.

Non-technical clients can appreciate the capacities that Tableau offers for detailed parsing, for example, dashboard advancement, and so forth., without inside and out preparation. Nonetheless, to get into the arrangement's capacities, more profound Data is an absolute necessity. Additionally, the nearby inclusion of IT pros is a need if an organization tries to grow the arrangement's usefulness.

* ***High Performance***

Aside from its high Visualization usefulness, clients rate its general execution as vigorous and dependable. The instrument additionally works quickly even on enormous Data, which makes its incredible execution a significant point in the rundown of the upsides of Tableau.

Multiple Data Source Connections

The product bolsters building up associations with numerous Data sources, for example, <u>HADOOP</u>, SAP and DB Technologies, which improves Data investigation quality and empowers the making of a bound together, instructive dashboard. Such a dashboard awards access to the necessary data for any client.

- ***Thriving Community and Forum***

The number of Tableau fans who put their aptitude and abilities in the network increments relentlessly. Business clients can amplify their insight on Data parsing and detail and get numerous valuable bits of knowledge in this network. Likewise, gathering guests are prepared to help settle any client issues and to share their experience.

- ***Mobile-Friendliness***

Also, the last one in our rundown of center Tableau benefits, there is a proficient portable application accessible for IOS and Android. It adds versatility to Tableau clients and enables them to keep insights readily available, just as it bolsters full usefulness that a Desktop and Online renditions have.

- ***Direct connection***

Tableau associates the clients straightforwardly to databases, Data stockrooms and different wellsprings of Data. It doesn't require any convoluted arrangement.

- ***Deals with big data***

Tableau can examine huge Data easily and envision it superior to some other DVT.

- ***Publishing and sharing***

The dashboard can be distributed live on the stage from which the client is getting to it. The outcomes can likewise be shared live.

- *Trending in the market*

Tableau is developing quickly in the business examination advertisement. It is being utilized in all ventures now. Many tops of the line organizations like Microsoft, Nokia, and Deloitte use Tableau to meet their business knowledge prerequisites.

- *Interactive visualizations*

One of the most significant highlights of Tableau is its capacity to make progressively delightful Data representations types. It produces appealing and utilitarian representations that will help the client in deciding.

- *Smart Maps*

Tableau additionally gives you a chance to look in the guide or rope Data focuses. It will find a solution to the land question "***Where***?"

- *Works across multiple platforms*

Tableau can be gotten to by the clients through the work area, program, iPad or cell phone. By this component, it has made an upheaval in the Data examination industry.

- *Copying between dashboards*

Tableau gives you a chance to duplicate the worksheets or any dashboard components between various exercise manuals. Given this element, you need not begin everything from scratch on the off chance that you have diverse business experts utilizing the Data representation types programming. You can likewise have consistent collaborations between the dashboards.

- *64-bit version*

Tableau gives you an alternative to pick between 32 pieces or a 64-piece variant. The rendition downloaded relies upon the OS. In a 32 piece OS, you can introduce just the 32-piece adaptation of Tableau. The 64-piece variant has a ton of memory space and improves the speed.

- *SAML Authentication*

SAML validation gives a client a chance to make a solitary sign-on in a blended framework condition. This will let the Tableau server to blend into your center business zones and inside applications.

- *Metadata Management*

Tableau gives you a chance to rename the fields and adjust the configurations rapidly and effectively. You can likewise make subsets of Data by choosing gatherings of focuses.

Some Amazing Tips for Using Tableau Data Visualizations

- *Keep it clean*

The dashboard highlight makes it simple for clients to make perplexing, intuitive Visualizations, consolidating various illustrations. At the point when done effectively, this can be an incredibly helpful device for business examiners to depict Data in a decipherable configuration. Be that as it may, over and over again these dashboards can get jumbled and hard to comprehend.

Diminishing title message and evacuating rehashed words can be a simple method to do this. Another straightforward change is to feature the significant actualities/figures and present these at the top so the watcher can see the significant Data straight away.

- *Sensible color choice*

This one sounds sufficiently basic, yet you'd be astonished. Insufficient hues and the representation can seem dull and un-connecting with, however too many can have the contrary impact and may seem amateurish.

- *Clear typography and simple labeling*

Utilizing reasonable, well-differentiated typography and basic naming is imperative for any Visualization. Tableau enables you to revise the typography effectively. A valuable component is the capacity to change the textual style on any individual piece of the diagram, from the pivot to the mark, to the title. An outsider device, for example, WebAim's shading contrast checker can be advantageous in guaranteeing the shading plan and text style you are utilizing has an adequate differentiation.

- *Use Tableau marks to show more variables*

Frequently you will need to show more than one variable in a diagram, without utilizing a shading angle like our bar graph model prior. We could utilize a dissipated diagram for two factors, however, shouldn't something be said about on the off chance that we have three? Continuing with our previous model, on the off chance that we needed to show several Github submits and stars just as donors, we could utilize Tableau's 'size' device to show this. Like with shading, straightforward drag the applicable measurement/measure onto the size symbol. The dissipate chart underneath shows this Data now, Github submitted by donors, with the size of the circle speaking to the number of stars it has.

- *Collaborate*

The last, and maybe most significant hint, is to utilize the regularly developing Tableau people group to team up and share your work with others. Obviously, on the off chance that you are entrusted with making something for your association that contains private data, at that point this doesn't concern you. In any case, for any non-touchy Data, use Tableau Public with the goal that others can see and gain from your work. Moreover, utilize the asset to get new thoughts and defeat hindrances that you might be confronting.

Conclusion On Tableau Data Visualizations

Tableau, with its ever-evolving set of features and updates is making it provide real and meaningful insights from data. It also comes with a very easy drag-drop interface that makes it easy to learn and in creating compelling, interactive dashboard-style reports and thus acts as a market leader in Data Visualization.